DRACOPIS

dp

PRESS

Swedish Poetry Nowadays

Johannes Anyuru
Eva-Stina Byggmästar
Naima Chahboun
Martin Högström
Freke Räihä
Matilda Södergran

An Anthology
of 6 poets in the 21st Century

Translated by
Kristian Carlsson

ISBN 978-91-87341-09-0

Dracopis_007
Swedish Poetry Nowadays; An Anthology of 6 Poets in the 21st Century
First edition. All rights reserved.

BY   Johannes Anyuru, Eva-Stina Byggmästar, Naima Chahboun
     Martin Högström, Freke Räihä, Matilda Södergran
&   Translated by Kristian Carlsson
⁋   Published by Dracopis Press, Malmö, Sweden, 2016
⁋   EUROPE: Printed by Lightning Source, UK, 2016
⁋   USA: Printed by Lightning Source, USA, 2016
©   2016: The writers & the translator

→   www.dracopis.com
⇆   beard@dracopis.com

Swedish Poetry Nowadays

Anthology
6 Poets
21st Century

Johannes Anyuru

Johannes Anyuru (b. 1979) lives in Gothenburg. He is a critically acclaimed writer of poetry and prose. Already in his first poetry collection, *Det är bara gudarna som är nya* [Only the gods are new] (Norstedts Förlag, 2003), he introduced his style of a harsh reality and lucid fiction, or the other way around. *Städerna inuti Hall* [Cities Inside the Hall Prison] (Norstedts Förlag, 2009) was his breakthrough third poetry collection, nominated to Augustpriset, the Swedish Publishers' Association's award for best book of the year. In the most recent years he has published mainly prose, which also became his international breakthrough and rendered him even more awards.

Table of contents

From *Städerna inuti Hall* (2009)
[Cities Inside the Hall Prison]
Publisher: Norstedts Förlag

Eva-Stina Byggmästar

Eva-Stina Byggmästar (b. 1967) is a Finno-Swedish poet born in Jakobstad in the west of Finland. Having spent several years in Sweden, she is now living in Finland again. She is a heartily playful poet, who has published about twenty books and been awarded several distinguished poetry prizes since her debut in 1986. *Men hur små poeter finns det egentligen* [But How Tiny Poets Are There After All] (Söderström & C:o / Wahlström & Widstrand, 2008) was nominated to Augustpriset, the Swedish Publishers' Association's award for best book of the year. In the recent decade she has published a new book almost annually.

Table of contents

From *Men hur små poeter finns det egentligen* (2008)
[But How Tiny Poets Are There After All]
Publisher: Söderström & C:o / Wahlström & Widstrand

Naima Chahboun

Naima Chahboun (b. 1980) lives in Stockholm. She has up till now only published one book, *Okunskapens arkeologi* [The Archaeology of Ignorance] (Norstedts Förlag, 2011), and it was awarded the *Katapult*-prize for best debut by the Swedish Writers Union. Besides her politically-sensitive writings, also manifested in magazine contributions, she is a Ph.D. student in Political Science at Stockholm University.

Table of contents

From *Okunskapens arkeologi* (2011)
[The Archaeology of Ignorance]
Publisher: Norstedts Förlag

Martin Högström

Martin Högström (b. 1969) lives in Stockholm. His typographical quest *Transfutura* (OEI Editör, 2005) was awarded the *Katapult*-prize for best debut by the Swedish Writers Union. It was followed by *Kommande industrilandskap* [Forthcoming Industrial Landscapes] (OEI Editör, 2007) and *Fängelsepalatset* [The Prison Palace] (OEI Editör, 2010). Högström aims for perfection in the sculptural sense of a poem and attaches great weight to the components of language. He has published a handful of books.

Table of contents

Freke Räihä

Freke Räihä (b. 1978) lives in Degeberga in the South of Sweden. He is a, mainly conceptual, poet, who also indulges himself with essayism and borderline prose. In 2001 he debuted with the poetry collection *Po-etik* [Po-etics] (Serum Förlag). In both *Konceptbeläggning: sjokkok* [Conceptual Coating: The Bulk Digest] (Tillexempel Förlag, 2010) and *Standardformulär för språkförbittring* [Standard Form for Language Resentment] (King Ink, 2011) there is a conceptual incentive that has chiseled the poetry. In recent years Räihä seems to accomplish the publication pace of two books annually.

Table of contents

Matilda Södergran

Matilda Södergran (b. 1987) is a Finno-Swedish poet. She grew up in Korsnäs in the west of Finland and is now living in Malmö, Sweden. She debuted in 2008 with the critically acclaimed *Hon drar ådrorna ur* [She pulls the Veins Out of] (Schildts). Södergran opens strange worlds in her writings, where the human body is always in some state of despair. *Maror (ett sätt åt dig)* [Hagridden (A Way for You)] (Schildts & Söderströms, 2012), her third poetry collection, can be read as a continuation of the narrative in her debut. She has published a handful of books.

Table of contents

Johannes Anyuru

Page 15-28

Poems from *Städerna inuti Hall* (2009)

[Cities Inside the Hall Prison]

¶

Fluorescent July
Paper walls, lit through
by ruthless

nylon sunshine

Property
is dead man's
waste

Most of all I
want: A best friend,
a boy writes
in a book, in another
city He doesn't
know you ought to
write Peace on Earth

He is the bus stop, fragment
of scratched glass He can't find
himself In another city far away
a body staggers, also looking
for its own life That was
on allowing it to touch
the... endless... morning light
immovable as marble, crowding sparrows
climb the wire netting, small hirsute
mice, grey substance, brain cells, they swirl
across the dust on a test pattern, from
loudspeakers a modem
chirps

The key is under the pot
in the backyard

He reads about one of the codes—Lucifer—
used on The Net He runs
further and further away,
motionless
As he wants to
disappear He reads
about newer codes, with open
keys
Quantum keys Bodies slither
in the sand, in front of
the wall Wide lips
parted, empty, to say
his name, then sink
into the wall's matter of aged
code, antiquated
keys, and get exterminated,
phantoms
they are saved,

appear
anew,

store signs
flicker
in the summer night,

cracked
amphorae,

the stamp
put to the upper side
of the metal piece, and it was engraved by
a hammer-blow—

Caught by the police for the first time
in adulthood, he
cries
fuck the law

Busy pain responses
by the cracked
concrete walls

Then there can't be a
first time The muscles are threaded
in line, and on
straw, and are marked
by weariness, damages, and concentric
pain, song, and they move about,
and are being moved about, as a Pavlovian
expansion, stretched,
the skin does its work,
by beauty, smoothness,
law, by fire, it is on fire He is the
sunspots of eyes He collapses
in the hot
ashes Grey clouds are puffing
between houses The animal
evolves from being part of a herd
as wolves and rats
to being an animal
lighting fires, as wasps,
termites, corals...

LETHE

Residential blocks
rising for miles as translucent
honeycombs,
swaying
in the hot, ash grey
morning
He bends
down washes himself
by the light Screws and nails rustle
across the floor
The buildings
are covered in skin
The sundews make the skin hirsute
A body stands
by the window, to look
at the sea It pokes
the wall
Microscopic beads of chitin
burst when hairs are
touched An ultra sharp
silicon tip advances
to inject
ugliness He bends
down, for
ever, got
so sad,
slowly disappears, a thin
crust crawling
away The purchase price
was fixed at a certain
quantity of
metal The blood of

the wild beast Grey
summer nights He's thinking
of us Cement powder
blown over the sea
The pots are holes he
moves about to avoid
moving away Trees are swaying
in the holes, lights He picked up
coins in the street
today Eyelids,
raggedy skin and globes
gathered in a new luminous
knot, a
dream, a
he

who arises
His hair sways
upwards, static, he weighs
the heavy
glass jar full of
pennies quarters

The drop telling us
about the ocean

¶

A young girl plays the hollow metal
receptacle shaped as a saucer, crouching
by a wall

The squad car stops, rotates
unfolding
into a corridor
of glimmering
mirrors

The global state of violence
is the hollow core
of existence

¶

Lowers the park bench into the sea, an atmosphere of Jovian planets,
splintered crystal, tear gas—

He is the tongs flying over the city, light of dawn breaking through
the clouds—

Someone places a container in front of a parked truck and prevents
the driver from continuing his work after the unloading,

"foot soldier of the future—a high tech monster"

A radar capable of discovering airplanes
far beyond the horizon—

The soul must bear the pressure of a billion atmospheres

Light—exceed!—burn!—seas have dried up—trees
fly over the city—tang—

¶

Perhaps the method of investigation itself
influences the sequences of dreams

¶

If you keep
your shyness and sense of shame
and in the subconsciousness of sleep know
you are being watched

The snow is
mustard gas

and animal teeth

Sitting on the bench
he's touching his naked
chest It was a
shore Shimmering
shards crunch
against the pier, hammered
stamps, king
responsible of weight,
substance, for each
piece—

The snow is
black, snow

of holes An animal of snow
lumbers in the hallways
all hundreds of thousands
of miles This animal
brings shadows, it shines darkly
in the dark does lit
up all hundreds of thousands
of cells

¶

He wraps a large
polygonal stone
in diapers, puts on tiny
mittens

The law devours
the stone

Thought it to
be food

¶

He leans backwards in the backseat
of the car Gold watches, diamond necklaces
drift weightless
in the river of light from headlights, scratch
the silver paint Wooden chips
get stuck in the facial
cloth The sensation that all the
people, all the objects, here,
are worn out, used
somewhere else already

That the bodies are made of
foam rubber, wax,

that a single particle
from a younger universe
would sink straight through
anything at all
concrete
steel

The summer
howls from within, hollow

The city doesn't present
life or death
but survival

He steps out of the car, cries are
echoing between balconies

Just
eyes visible, red

hysterical—

They are
many

Batman is unique
in a sense
besides
the huge fortune
he has no super powers

He is the sneakers
sticky from blood

I'm
not black
at all

I just wear a black
ski mask

The French torturer
tortured his wife and children as well

Got sand in his eyes

¶

Arc lamps sway on the necks
of herons,

leafs blow in
from the sea, back into
the highway

If he tries to kill himself
I'll just bare myself
so that he can't

Calculating

He lies
in a receptacle, plays
hide and seek

That's how to set out
for the heart of light
on a dark vessel

¶

Slaughterous whiteness of stripped depots
wobbles in the squad car side mirrors
Clattering, echoing
sounds Airports, construction
sites, plastics, lights Dogs that eat
the hair on the mannequins

Graveless and forlorn
are the ones that stay behind

Blades of knives dangle
as diamond earrings
from his hollow
eye sockets

Ammonia
sprayed by the wind
patters
on the tarpaulin,

what is dying cries out its
death, blowing

dyingly
over cities,

sea of
stairs

Eva-Stina Byggmästar

Page 33-43

Poems from *Men hur små poeter finns det egentligen* (2008)

[But How Tiny Poets Are There After All]

¶

heartish beat of consonants,
that's good... the vowels hover
above our heads in a very
delightful manner...

—

UPPER-CASE MOON LIGHT
TIME NOW FLOWS CALMLY
IN DRESSING GOWN STILL
WRITING-PAD IN THE HAND
PENCIL STUMP BEHIND THE EAR
THE DAY MAY BEGIN
THE LIFE OF A POET.

¶

you want. to have, a den for the lyrical... I'll
give it to you. oh, you're a poetry-fox. look
at the rowanberries shining above us, they
are tiny lanterns, tiny but beautiful. look,
it was my bit. of luck. she said, this poem
I have written with the feather of a magpie.
I answered, but the blooming giant sunflower
touches all chords on my little harp, and this
house resembles, if not a heart, at least
a book.

¶

very pleased
with *the leaves*, they do conceal
well. the poems cover *the leaves*,
from edge to edge and beyond,
pass into the other side softly
with graceful delicate strokes...

that's how the bookworms made
hardback treehouses, out of books they
made homely environments, wonderfully
beautiful, for the petite typists.

¶

but the tiny-books-of-poetry, so
easy to take along on forest walks,
then further and further up... and you
and the poem are, no doubt, much alike,
but how tiny indeed, the dwarf birch,
a miniature entirely, although a birch,
with the nearly elliptical leafs it pressed
itself against the heart, soft as a writing-pad.

¶

my wilderness poets, I'm feeding them with blueberry
porridge, they like that—yes, I was like a mother to them.
but poets, if they existed. live, in small. houses, their
sofas ought to be comfy. and pillows, should actually
look like sunflowers or only be reminding of pine cones
but poets should be, tiny! as we are more fond of the
tiny ones, we reckon they are very handy to carry along
on forest walks, to and fro, but over all doglike tiny,
or hamsterlike they write, while we're handing them
writing-pad after writing-pad and then they read
densly written poems for the sun with their too big
front teeth, but we appreciate them, we think they
are beautiful, they are somewhat pretty, they look
like soft toys, they also make us slightly poetic—

¶

they collapse, these eccentrics with their soft spot for poetry
they collapse into a pile inside the door, so you yell strike!
and then, shortly afterwards, you welcome them in, but
then they just rush to the small writing desks and become
a delightful starting block crowding, and they ask to be
allowed to commence on the spot with the devoted compiling
of the dearest of names, the favorite name, the most wonderful,
the altogether sun-and-moon-like name, the name of my dove.

¶

the paper swallow
could be some kind of new winter bird—
which, as poets, only hides in
libraries and book stores... far into
the most verbose alcoves, in a crevice,
soft... and, with the badgering loaded
with capital letters, then to be carried like...
like this all the way to...

g-l-i-m-m-m-m-ering stars!

we were intoxicated by these snow-poems,
but that's how we'll have our alphabetical presence
over and over again! oh look, indeed a new poetry-moon
night after night over those rows of books, going on for miles—

¶

when time comes the pretty leaves of grass extend
themselves and crooked stars sparkle in the corner of
the eye, then you merely want to think about the wool
think about a green spot about beautiful small forests
think about tender cries from fairy tale birds want to think
about how to set out upon the gangway with a spate of
words in the back and HEAVEN'S LIBRARIAN—
THE CRANE carrying such dainty chapbooks of poetry to
such solid reading desks and the tiny chapbooks goes well
there all the while... chimes from the scents of water are heard
quite near and the plantain and the chamomile are swaying
gently and calmly in the breeze as to here below create a
narrow space, unshadowed......... but open to starglare...—

O WONDERFULLY ONE DAY ALL
OF US WILL BE LIBRARIANS BUT
HOW COULD EVERYTHING
ALL OF A SUDDEN BECOME SO
POETIC OR HOW TINY POETS
ARE THERE AFTER ALL—

Poetry factory #153

Well, loveliest is the morning shift, as the
pencil subcontractor makes his appearance
with a wheelbarrow and, breathing a sigh
of relief, heaves off the newly sharpened ones.
On the coffee break a fellow worker and I get
up on to the roof of the Poetry Factory and look
upon the world—indeed we do this every day
rain or shine, we stand there quietly for a while
with our hands in our dungarees, respectively,
and inhale the oxygen while synchronically
thinking: so that is how it appears today—
the world, it is here, it exists today
as well—but only when the weather is fine
we bring our thermoses and biscuits, sitting here
considering and considering our decent lives
and how come we are the ones working here
as poets—no idea.

Back on the factory floor we hear the
beautiful thumpadump of machinery, this
is just like Santa's workshop almost to the
letter, the caps are all that's missing,
in the winter not even that. so why
shouldn't we be pleased—

Here you also enter dictionaries, whole lines out
of context or just the capital letters, sometimes
a complete flora, thus a bit of everything enters
the tape in the machine, then you turn a winch,
round and round. and shift to a higher gear. when
all is finished collections of poetry are lined up

in row after row after row after row, it is particularly
beautiful.

Then it's time to clock out and once more ride
your bike home to the well-made bed of the
kitchen sofa, and a little dog—well, you consider
it to be all together decent and while you're
preparing some oatmeal and night is drawing
on the world you think about how tiny the letters
could become before they actually disappear.

¶

the florists went no doubt with the floras their
own ways for the sake of the beautiful nature,
brought also life-size flowers, but at last it was
said that enough's enough, it will be just like
a jungle! and then they said, fine, that's how
we wanted it to be from the very first moment,
but are there really no taller sunflowers, 16 feet
can't be regarded as tallness for a little flower
and we want the wind to be soughing through
them—yes, does it do that, it does, I see, and
is it possible to put canopy swings in them now,
it is. in deed—but is it possible also to have
meadows of daisies or might a garden seem too
pink and poets waltz around there, for real, and
can you let them get lost in the jungle garden
can you let them find their way home again to
their beautiful hazel mouse-fashioned homes and
on the courtyard, then, allow them to recite their
own wilderness poetry to a lovely crowd of
gigglish little dogs... Huh?

Naima
Chahboun

Page 47-61

Poems from *Okunskapens arkeologi* (2011)

[The Archaeology of Ignorance]

¶

if the purpose of a map is to make the surrounding world comprehensible by diminishing it removing a dimension & reduce its elements to a limited collection of manageable symbols the orienteer has a bird's-eye view of ("von oben") then the purpose of a conspiracy (i.e. any theory) is to simplify a complex & aimless reality by streamlining & overstating the causal connections that the brain constantly tries to clarify in consequence of a genetic code which in its turn is in consequence of thousands of generations having bred characteristics that serve the survival which in its turn is in consequence of the conditions of life which in its turn is an issue for philosophy the imagination that gave the human kind means to create her own opportunities is also the origin of the paranoia the paradise the proof of god's existence the wooden horse of TROY the infinite combinations that give rise to fusion fission fiction

let the record state: (F) FAR-REACH-ING questions the FORMULATIVE

privilege of PHYSICS & FINANCES the FOLLOWERS the FRACTIONS the FRIC-TION surface between the PHANTOM pain of the FOSSILIZED society & the FRAYED FLEET of cars of the FOREMOST social movements the FREONS the PHRENOLOGY the FULL FRONTAL collision with the FUTURE FAST FORWARDING

already (in 1940) before the war comes across the ATLANTIC an on-screen introduction is given to the miraculous weapon that at once makes the US undefeatable & guarantees world peace it is starring RONALD R who's transition to a political career takes off when he develops disgust at Communism & in the already strike-affected HOLLYWOOD of the 40's becomes an FBI informant & president of the Screen Actors Guild which ETHEL dreamt to be part of when she went around on various talent hunts in her youth to sing her only song

a bombshell
a one hit wonder

a barely visible foot print on the

time axis of opinions about the
future a half-ape crawling out at
first submissively crouched then
combative with prominent chest
& finally perfectly erected the
wobbling balance act of history
(HOMO HABILIS HOMO ERECTUS HOMO
HERO HERO HERO) could at any mo-
ment end up on its rear end

HO HO HO

the importance of readiness (duck
& cover when the siren sounds) &
of calculation (how many political
doctrines can fit under a single
umbrella?) are stressed in the
incessant evacuation exercises
the hoarding of eatables the
all-inclusive cover up of the
authorities the judicial system &
all other public sectors & are non
the least demonstrated by the city
set-up built in the desert to put
the resisting power of modern life
to the test in regards to nuclear
attacks & by means of film convey
the results to the population

experiment NO. I: a decayed
branch on the pine tree BILL has
neglected to prune is cut off by
the blast wave & falls into the
nursery LIZZY immediately departs
this life & JONAH breaks his leg
MEGAN who at impact is in the
kitchen gets simultaneously hit

by a flying serving dish left un-
washed on the dining table & now
becoming her fate BEN who slept
peacefully in her arms tumbles
through the air & ends up on his
head cracking his skull against
the polished kitchen marble floor
which is then covered by blood
& brain tissue at the sight of the
accident BILL falls on his knees
crying sure he doesn't no not BILL
BILL carries JONAH in his strong
arms staggers (he is hurt) stands
up straight again & carries his son
towards the air-raid shelter at the
neighbors goes downstairs out into
the street onwards to the neigh-
boring lot but at the moment he
opens the fence gate the neighbor
is opening fire & BILL & JONAH are
shot to death (an act of self-defence
THE SUPREME COURT establishes
when they give their practice-
constituted ruling two years after
the impact of the bomb)

GAME OVER

let the record state: (G) GATE-
KEEPERS the GRATING in between
the GRAVEL of the GHETTO & the
GLASSED GEOMETRY of the GAL-
LERIA GALLERIES under GUISES the
long GONE songs the GUERRILLA
war spreading like GRASS roots
like GMO:s the GRADUALLY GLID-
ING GROUNDWORKS the GALAXIES

GRAVITATING towards something
GROUNDBREAKING

the epidemic subsequently named
the Orienteering Disease has its
first serious outbreak in the mid
90's when it day by day became
harder to separate the East from
the West but already (in 1945) the
strike breaking out in February
raises suspicion in the House of
Representatives about the most
westerly outpost of the West be-
ing on its way to glide into the
Eastern Hemisphere which in its
turn give rise to the founding of
THE HOUSE UN-AMERICAN ACTIVITIES
COMMITTEE (HUAC) who is given
the task of unmasking & crush-
ing subversive elements within
the independent department of
propaganda in HOLLYWOOD

remember: anti-Americanism also
comes from within the US

the first ones to be put on strike
are the set designers out of neces-
sity resulting in overtime for the
dramaturgists mammoth scenes
are cancelled more shots are done
outdoors history & adventure
yield to the favorable production
conditions of family drama: the
young couple who are separated
from their children due to a tes-
timony from the spiteful brother

of the wife her mother & siblings
taking sides against her the time
in prison the death sentence the
orphaned boys tossed between
orphanages & foster care one
(MICHAEL) being violent the other
(ROBERT) being withdrawn the
sturdy social worker who buys the
children a decent meal (ham-
burgers & soda) at their weekly
rendezvous a tragedy of per-
fect dimensions leaving each &
everyone misty-eyed +++++

the jury's award for Best Perfor-
mance goes to the infiltrator on
each side, who rise in the ranks
like rockets by surpassing their
ardorous antagonists in no time
the government spies become the
toughest demagogs of the Com-
munist party uncompromising
ideologists seeking out counter-
revolutionary elements to crush
with an iron fist mandating wild
strikes ruthlessly cracked down
on by the communist agents of
HUAC as a consequence the party
line radicalized further a farce in-
hibiting creativity by mid October
(1946) all shootings in color have
been stopped the studio crew can
barely separate black from white

but DAVID hardly notices any dif-
ference he is colorblind when the
defence asks him to describe the

roses climbing on the grey façade
at FOLEY SQUARE (FEDERAL COURT
HOUSE NEW YORK SOUTHERN DISTRICT)
he replies that the color indeed
has escaped him however he can
name everything that grows in the
flower bed

cosmos
garden party
love story
tornado
mayday
magna charta
belle époque
remember me

one out of a hundred flowers
each species divided into races
each race into classes each class
into households & families RUTH'S
bloated stomach grows faster by
the week the ultra sound vaguely
displays a grey lump

bird
or in between?
fish

let there be distinction between
what is falling down from the sky
& what is washed ashore from
the sea between assault & enter-
tainment the aesthetics of paired
opposites: public housing projects
vs. television soaps coverall vs.
all inclusive unisex vs. sex appeal

(shortly after the nuclear testings
in the pacific atoll named BIKINI a
two piece swimsuit with the same
name is presented for the first
time)

the offensive action named
Striker's Atom Bomb by the press
involves gathering in front of a
movie theater in time for the late
show giving away the murderer
(the murderer is the one least
expected) to young couples &
thrill seakers standing in line at
the counter the conflict continues
until November (1950) when an
alleviated J EDGAR H Director of
FBI archives the case & reaches
for a new file on his desk the one
where the title "ROSENBERG" will
be replaced with "crime of the
century"

the alluring epithet "the most
dangerous weapon of mankind"
however still lies with the pen
after twenty four months of dili-
gent efforts (1964) two American
postgraduate students in Physics
assigned by the government
managed to recreate the blue-
print for the hydrogen bomb
without other guidance than the
volumes supplied by their local
library the literary drive of the
strike committee aims firstly at
elevating the fighting spirit of the

workers & secondly at gaining public appreciation & assumes the shape of an offset pamphlet with the ten commandments of the strike

1. one man's loss is
another man's circuses
2. never was so little
owed by so many to so few
3. in Africa all cats are black
4. those who forget to repeat
are doomed to
go down to history
5. barbwire is always greener
on the other side
6. the freedom is different
for those who contemplate
7. the one sitting
under the glass roof
should throw the first stone
8. blood is thicker than water
but oil is thicker than blood
9. don't ask what your country
can do for you ask what it
can stop you from doing
10. have you got a light?

let the record state: (H) the HEATHEN engravings of HISTORY & HEROIC tales the HALF-LIFE of HUMANITARIAN HARDWARE the HYPNOSIS transforming HYSTERIA into HYPOCRISY HAIRSPLITTING into HIATUS the invisible HAND gripping your HEAD the HIDDEN HYPOTHESIS of the HARSH HOPE (a HERMETICALLY

sealed HERBARIUM in a constantly expanding void a HERMENEUTICALLY entangled explanation in a constantly expanding research lab)

experiment NO. 2: BILL lifts BEN up on his left arm & holds JONAH with his right hand JONAH holds LIZZY & thus together they go calm & composed down to the air-raid shelter BILL has built BILL lights the portable stove to make white beans in tomato sauce while the kids build huts out of cans & MEGAN hoovers the radioactive dust up with the new vacuum cleaner BILL has bought BILL wriggles out of his apron revealing a well ironed & spotless shirt beneath MEGAN's silk scarf which she pulls off & folds neatly her hair lies in immaculate golden curls mmm smells yummy JONAH says why can't it be nuclear war all the time LIZZY says MEGAN throws a glance at BILL & smiles

the end

the inevitable closing scene that always comes unexpectedly the little sting of disappointment when the theme song appears the reactions when the FBI agent descending from the television screen into the living room of JULIUS & ETHEL where MIKE & ROBBY are curled up in the couch turns

off the spy movie & delivers his
line ("you are under arrest") are
as chocking as European govern-
ments accusing the US for dump-
ing large quantities of low quality
movies all over the convalescent
continent during the hard times
after the war thereby twisting not
only internal competition but also
the citizens' conception of the
world with a mass-produced myth
about the unparalleled individ-
ual (hey DOLLY! hey DOLLY DOLLY
DOLLY!) unachievable dreams &
public lies

one size fits all
love at first sight
based on a true story

platitudes oozing all the way
down to the basement of SING-SING
the love letter ETHEL ends with
"see you in court darling"

let the record state: (I) the INSTANC-
ES of INDOCTRINATION the INVENTORY
of IDEAS & IMPULSES the INVERSION
of IDEOLOGIES the INSPECTIONS
INFECTIONS INJECTIONS of ISOLATES
the INSTRUMENTAL INHIBITION of the
INTERN'S ILLUSORY IDENTITY

the particular ID-tags US autho-
rities hand out in case a family
member should be separated from
the others at a nuclear disaster

are as effective as the name tags
all passengers are asked to put
fully visible on their luggage
right before the train takes off
to the secluded resorts with the
memorable names SACHENHAUSEN
BERGEN-BELSEN AUSCHWITZ-BIRKENAU
& as insightful as the suicide pre-
vention programme which after
a notorious hanging at a peniten-
tiary in NORRTÄLJE (2008) where
the staff leaves the internee in the
noose until a doctor reaches the
location & the attempt advances
to a completed suicide has all the
first aid kits in Swedish prisons
equipped with pruning shears

(silence)

then finally being neglected by
audience strained filmmakers in-
vent the test screenings to decide
from the result which of the three
different endings will end up in
movie theatres the sad one the
happy one & the puzzling one are
screened one after another to the
focus group & the participants are
filled with unexpected sense of
responsibility filling out the ballot
& putting it in the urn the result
is evident facing the choice be-
tween yes or no a clear majority
of the respondents answer may-
be & thus graciously evades the
stranglehold of binary opposites

facing more stable isotopes (the development tendency the phase out-scenario the consensus solution the psychologically edifying biodegradable compromise)

remaining questions: what is cause? what is effect? what is someone else's headache? not until months after the FBI has handed the ROSENBERG case over to the district attorney DAVID's ad is discovered the one he has been instructed to place in the weekend supplement of a well known newspaper should he ever be in need of help to escape

"you are a young man in the middle of your career you have engineering education & ambitions above average but mediocre income you are unfit to be a leader but by no means a recluse you easily approach people to have a chat you are persevering but can easily keep quiet as well if needed you do have an eye for details you are able to memorize a thirty eight-digit number sequence for at least four weeks after having it read to you just once a striking feature in you is the ability to gain people's trust ever so often strangers stop you in the street to reveal their most intimate secrets or tell you their life stories several times

you have left strangers behind crying at train stations or hotel bars whilst you scurried along to your destination despite that these people feel (but you don't know it if you never share your name & number) a deep gratitude toward you almost borderlining sacred worship when they in their most agonizing & joyous moments in life think back on your short but clearly crucial meeting you yourself are suspicious toward strangers & since childhood you have only had a few (if any) profound relationships without exception you are faithful to your ideals reply to: a new beginning?"

experiment NO. 3: for weeks BILL MEGAN JONAH BEN & LIZZY are patiently waiting in the air-raid shelter but the nuclear attack never comes in stead the enemy is falling apart due to internal discrepancies & budget deficit out of basements garages & toolsheds the ones in hiding come crawling drowsily they blink at the sun & then astonishingly regard the distant rainbow BILL's overgrown beard the withered lawns someone burst into laughter another one follows & a third a fourth the laughter spreads across the block past the freeways over to the suburbs out into the countryside &

across the oceans the whole world
is laughing hitting their thighs
with the palms of their hands
ready to split their sides jumping
up & down gasping for air until
they fall dead on the ground the
last word to be panted out before
the convulsive laughter fades is
LIZZY'S

why?

the credit titles roll thanks to
ETHEL JULIUS MICHAEL & ROBERT
ROSENBERG RUTH & DAVID GREEN-
GLASS ANNE & ABEL MEEROPOL HARRY
GOLD J EDGAR HOOVER NIELS BOHR
GALILEO GALILEI RONALD REAGAN JO-
SEPH STALIN ANATOLY YAKOVLEV STAN-
ISLAV PETROV ERWIN SCHRÖDINGER
NICOLAUS COPERNICUS HAROLD C UREY
IVAN PAVLOV IRVING KAUFMAN ALBERT
EINSTEIN GARRETT HARDIN CHARLIE
CHAPLIN HENRY DALE THOMAS HOBBES
& THOMAS EDISON no animals were
harmed during the production
all rights reserved for somebody
higher in the sinuous spiral stair-
case of genetics (survival of the
spin-off)

¶

previously: by coincidence (a
clash of at least two independent
causal chains) the Universe has
appeared by coincidence the
Earth has assumed favorable
conditions for life a selection of
random micro-organisms multi-
plied & evolved into fish which
by coincidence evolved into
tadpoles which by coincidence
evolved into dinosaurs which by
coincidence became extinct &
allowed for a random assembly
of mammals to have supremacy
& evolve into human beings
a coincidental sidestep mildly
overlooked by the experiencedly
observing nature

one time is no time

if depicting the age of Earth
by twelve hours humanity has
only existed for one fortieth of a
second & any moment (tick-tock)
the clock is striking twelve the
unyielding end & starting point
when hours & minutes & seconds
coincide in a vertical line & time
starts anew as if nothing had hap-
pened a revolution in the proper

sense of the word: to turn 360°
start over return to the beginning

re-voltere

(Latin) to turn 360° start over
return to the beginning as if
nothing had happened but which
beginning? the LOWER EAST SIDE
childhood the crowded drafty &
dark apartment the logic conflicts
(moral-philosophic socioeconom-
ic) the lodging people (prostitu-
tes) the psychosexual stages the
heritage of Orthodox Judaism
singing lessons rabbinical school
the first love that also became the
last the awakening (political) re-
lated to advancements of fascism
in EUROPE? or even earlier to the
discovery & conquest of AMERICA
being the beginning of a ground-
breaking globalization of plants
animals & people culminating in
HAWAII (folded with extra cheese)
& laying the foundations of MUSEO
DE CULTURAS POPULARES E INDÍGENAS?
or earlier still to the empty sheet
of prehistory the first staggering
steps of the naked ape leaving
the sun-drenched nudist beach

of EDEN & tens of thousands of generations later returning with flippers & firearms

re-volver

a shot being fired brushing against the carotid artery of Western civilization to then (by free will or without external cause) change direction & hit the dispatcher who by dismayed cries illustrates the trajectory

let the record state: (o) the OR-GANIZED OMENS OCCURRENCES the OBLITERATED OPEN-hearted ONES the OUT OF the ORDINARY OPEN-heart surgery the OVERTURE of autopsy the OVERT ORATIONS the OVATIONAL public OPINION the OPIUM of OBJEC-TIVITY

independent observers confirm that the information JULIUS & ETHEL are considered to have communicated is of no value to the military power of the USSR firstly the technology is already known through other sources secondly the designs reconstructed for the prosecution on the whole are incomprehensible DAVID leaves the POLYTECHNIC INSTITUTE OF BROOKLYN (in 1940) failing all subjects (drawing included) however the scientists who plead for his

death sentence to be revoked are all the more well-reputed ALBERT E & HAROLD C U a chemist who had participated in building the bomb & who later would lay the foundations of the so called cosmochemistry on behalf of which NASA (in 2001) launches the GENESIS probe towards the sun

hasta la vista

a single bombing plane was spotted over NAGASAKI & this time not loaded with leaflets telling people what will come if they won't overthrow the Emperor immediately & surrender to their opponents ("ask anybody from HIROSHIMA") this time the plane suddenly sheers & drops two million dollars worth of leading-edge technology over the thousand year old Japanese civilization

it resembles something
it resembles chaos

it resembles the whorehouse POMPEII that keeps its orgies in the dark for seventeen centuries like a roar of laughter under the ashes from VESUVIO a womb of civilization chocking the Victorian era archaeologists distorted bodies forever stagnated in unmentionable positions the peculiar facial expressions the merged groins the daisy chain

did this happen? did the sun disappear as if it was put inside a trash bag? was as much as a third of the surface seawater mixed with blood? did the sky turn completely silent for about half an hour? did thousands of people die from contaminated water? did someone really say "the civilians are **eradicated** from now on we are all soldiers"?

the bacteria which by mutation will cause Orienteering Disease becomes known at the turn of the century as Trench Fever symptoms appear when combatant units carrying out innumerable diversions & relocations loose sight of the front line the difference between enemy & allied home & away being wiped out in the neutral mess apparently covering each & every no man's land until someone gazes at the lit compass of the MILKY WAY & realizes that the whole firmament is pivoted

twinkle twinkle

GENESIS bursts through the legendary membrane of the atmosphere & disappears into the claustropho-

bia of empty space the increasingly desperate dream of bumping into a surface the search in vacuum for something that can be called intelligence behind closed doors the office of THE INTELLIGENCE continuously enters & decodes the data the generous generator is randomizing letter denotations at the same speed as the bipolar world produces diagnoses in no time the department's numerous desk drawers have brought forth three similar systems for analyzing the world around us

1. SWOT
(strengths weaknesses
opportunities & threats)
2. PEST
(politics economy social
factors & technology)
&
3. STEEP
(ditto but with the addition
of environment)

the climatology takes its vengeance in the greenhouse: the White man's fertile flower box contravenes the Asian man's pile of brushwood reeking of charcoal & the relentless fighting spirit characterizing populations near oil deposits fishing-boats are sunken outside the European coast when the quota is filled

let the record state: (P) the PAPER
tigers of the PORTFOLIO the PARA-
GRAPHS the PRIORITIES the PROFILES
the PROFIT the POSTHUMOUS PUBLICA-
TION of the PARTING julius & ethel
— PR or PC? POLEMICS versus PATHOS
PUBLICLY versus POLITICALLY the
PACIFYING PRIVATIZATIONS versus the
PANDEMIC PRACTICE of PIRATE copies

postscript: file after file after file
baked into cream cakes & from
the inside dividing them in parts
equal to the original whole the
paradigmatic shift of reproduc-
tion from the immaculate certifi-
cate of the Virgin Birth to the
illustrious Eden of ones & zeros
(computers surpassing humans
in checkers & chess but display-
ing considerably worse results in
everyday tasks such as preparing
a meal or changing diapers) the
rule is defined by the world of
research: the **exception** is
what is human

violated rules (steal stole stolen
hurt hurt hurt) vowel gradations
changing the melody unexpected
key change new stanzas in the
libretto of the Western World:

karaoke

kamikaze

origami

a thousand paper cranes dive
into MANHATTAN revenge aiming
at symmetry: balance on the one
hand terror on the other

the starting point seven to twelve
for the clock meant to adorn the
cover of BULLETIN OF THE ATOMIC
SCIENTIST & illustrate the hazard
of nuclear attacks is set without
considering anything but the
merely aesthetic (graphically
seven minutes equals about a
third of the golden angle that in
its turn equals about a third of a
full circle & derives from the pro-
portions some would say is divine
but others regard as a completely
irrational number)

question: was the motto "never a
war again after the bomb" over-
or underestimating the range of
rationality? firstly the contradic-
tions speak like several other ex-
agents DAVID & RUTH bear witness
to repeatedly receiving phone
calls & visits with regards "from
JULIUS" the statements are given
impartial to each other as well as
to the insistent assurances from
every interrogated witness that
contacts between network agents
without exceptions were made
under assumed names secondly
the years after the war ended have
their say the conscience of the

world arranging countless confer-
ences SWEDEN as a stockpile of
arms the readiness to compromise
characterizing the task to present
a treaty that will secure the sur-
vival of both humanity & war

the USSR carrying out its first
nuclear testings in August twenty
nine (1949) moves the hand of
the clock from seven (tick-tock)
to three minutes prior

let the record state: (Q) "the status
QUO of the cold war has put the
hurt nation in QUEST for a QUISLING
according to the theory that only
an American can create an atom
bomb & if anyone else creates
an atom bomb it will also be an
American (QUOD erat demonstran-
dum)"

ETHEL is looking around the hall
between the judge's bench & the
gallery there are three rows of
chairs the chief clerk sits on the
first one the district attorney sits
on the second one & the defense
sits on the one closest to the
gallery the jury box next to the
bench is placed with the inter-
rogator on the left & the witness
stand on the right so that the
members of the jury need to turn
their heads 180° for each question
answered

left-right

the map sifts the world through a
political or geographical grid
water is the only thing no inter-
pretation manages to disregard
dripping calmly on the top of the
head wearing away the thin sur-
face of ideologies methodically
eating its way through the earth
crust's skeleton reshaping the
landscape as its private network
of roads the map is redrawn: for
each standard there is another
standard just as each conception
of the world correspond to sharp
bladed custom made pincers
pressed against the horizons of
the temples the human brain at-
tempting to measure the human
brain

136   2.998   140.000   6.000.000
who's next?

the empathic skills are in inverse
proportion to the number of vic-
tims it is easy to feel sympathy for
a single martyr but compassion
is already decreasing before the
second one & the more death tolls
are rising a lesser degree of identi-
fication is reached heading for the
mass-medial solipsism of the zero
point life after life after life piled
high in anonymous graves women
children & slaves of the statistics

people never forced to ask them-
selves what they will do with
seven hundred virgins

let the record state: (R) the
RETROACTIVE RUBRICAL RECOGNI-
TION RIDDLES REHEARSED REPLIES
the REQUISITE territory the REALITY
of editors RETREATING before the
RECREANT RHETORICS of RABID RAC-
ISTS the ROPE TRICK the RECIPES ten
easy steps to serfdom (a REFORM
program for REVOLUTIONARIES)

the rigid somersault of progress
large-scale manufacture closing
the circle around production &
consumption in the same way as
genetic engineering completes
the fusion of nature & popular
culture which commenced in
the early Romanticism with the
electric figment of FRANKENSTEIN's
imagination the re-distributional
politics of fictional seed coats:
even those who won't sow shall
reap the barren fruits of the tree
of science

strange fruit
united fruit

the perpendicular scars across
scorched soil in the allotment a
barely existent surface friction
where caravans of freight cars
bring democracy in & natural

resources out the filthy mission
of civilization: to make gentle-
men out of head-hunters & vice
versa

vis-à-vis & reverse visit & contro-
versy commercial transactions
& transformations electrons
speeding in a beeline between
two opposite poles the currents
of the alternating & the direct
respectively the interdependence
the parallel lives deaths within
the interval of a few minutes
two shadows merged shoulder
to shoulder inseparable identical
the quiet prayer of the remaining
twin tower

one time is no time

DAVID asseverates when confront-
ed with RUTH's statement to their
lawyer the confession that her
husband already as a child had
difficulties with separating reality
from fiction that he hallucinated
got struck by panic that he had
"seen elephants" at several occa-
sions it was a long time ago & he
was ill you see the fever made him
delirious now on the other hand
he is quite certain that it was from
a source at GENERAL ELECTRICS JULIUS
stole the blueprint of a projected
space platform to be located be-
tween the earth & the moon

let the record state: (s) the termi-
nal STATE of STAR wars the SEVEN
STARRED SOURNESS in SOLAR plexus
the SUBLIME STANDSTILL the SUBLIMI-
NAL SUPREMACISTS the intersECTION
of SPOTLIGHTED SEGREGATION &
SOLIDARITY gala SOLO performances

JULIUS our man on the inside our
man in ALBUQUERQUE WASHINGTON
NEW YORK our man on the moon
(singing):

a little step
from the capital letter of the law
tight spacing
to be executive or to be executed
a cell is a cell is a cell
& so although many we
are one & the same body
as we all are part of the same
pueblo unido
ein VOLK ein REICH ein FÜHRER
not a glimpse
of red capes
of clenched fists
between the bars
SING-SING SING-SING
when will SUPERMAN come?

the persistent rumor that JOSEPH S
will send troops to rescue JULIUS
& ETHEL proves to be considerably
exaggerated while THE COMMITTEE
TO SECURE JUSTICE IN THE ROSENBERG
CASE gains support from provinces
further & further away the execu-

tion is creeping (tick-tock) closer
by the day

September eight (2004) the signal
is lost the probe goes astray rap-
idly loosing height it crashes into
the desert sand of UTAH unharmed
BILL climbs up from the debris
pulls his hand through his mop
of hair with a dazzlingly white
smile straight at the camera like
a gift from above like a deus ex
mac(c)hina a choir of angels sing-
ing in exelcis in absurdum in
absentia

one god is no god

a patrol is sent from the space
research laboratory in LOS ALAMOS
to recover & return the remnants
of the GENESIS fiasco

Martin Högström

Page 65-74
Poems from *Kommande industrilandskap* (2007)
[Forthcoming Industrial Landscapes]

Page 75-83
Poems from *Fängelsepalatset* (2010)
[The Prison Palace]

TWO MILLION FIVE HUNDRED AND SIXTY THOUSAND POEMS

*

A MUFFLED WHINE
NOTHING RESEMBLES ANYTHING
TO INVOICE: TO REVENGE
HORSES, COWS AND PIGS

*

A WIDE FOREST A DARK NIGHT
AN EVENT WITHOUT EFFICACY IN LANGUAGE
"TO WIN"
IT CAN ONLY BE EXAMINED AND DISCARDED

*

SÖDERTÄLJE APPEARS TO BE CLOSER TO STOCKHOLM
THAN THE OTHER WAY AROUND
EVERYBODY LIES
LAST WEEK, THIS WEDNESDAY AND NEXT FRIDAY

*

COMFORT, PASSION
A WEB OF DOUBLE NEGATIVES
A CERTAIN DISHONEST LONELINESS
THE WORLD IS (ALSO) TO NOT SEE

*

TO SEEK OUT A POINT
ONE MUST ACKNOWLEDGE A DISTANCE
I SEE YOU AS THE ARBITRARY SLIDE
THRU A DYNAMIC CATALOGUE OF PRONOUNS

*

A LITERAL SENSE, ON HOLD
YOU WISH FOR MORE, AND "LESS"
THE STORY OF YOUR LIFE
CARRIES AN ANNIHILATION MECHANISM

*

AN ABSOLUTE OBJECT
(SUBSTANCE OF PAIN)
LINES, RULES, TIME
TRUST IS THE GRAMMATICAL MODE OF EMOTION

*

A LACK OF TEMPER
THE CONVERSATION IS OVERLOADED
THE SLOW MUSCLES OF MY EYES
IMAGE BY IMAGE

*

THE SICKNESS AS A TALE OF DETAILS
AN INSECT, A BUG
THE NEEDS OF THE VULNERABLE ONES
ISOLATED IN LANGUAGE

*

FROM LEFT TO RIGHT
AND TO THE LINE BELOW
500 YEARS IS A SHORT PERIOD
BUT COME ON!

*

FOR NOW THE CHINK IN FRONT OF THE ROOM IS
THE ONLY SPACE AVAILABLE
HATRED & FOOD
THAT'S FUNDAMENTAL

*

A DISPROPORTIONATE EAGERNESS
CIRCUIT BY CIRCUIT
SOMEONE NAGGING
YOU WERE SOMEBODY ELSE THEN

*

IN SPEECH YOU OWN ME
(IN SILENCE AS WELL)
NOTHING BUT AGONY
ON THE OTHER SIDE OF THE PAGE

*

BLUE LIGHTS
THE RED AND GREEN MAN
WHO OR WHEN?
PLAN BETTER NEXT TIME

*

A DENSENESS
A DARKNESS, A LIGHT
REALLY, I DON'T MEAN A THING
THE 24TH OF JULY, 2036

*

FROM A DIRECT CONFRONTATION WITH SILENCE
MY STORY IS SHORT OF UNIVERSALITY
THE MAN GETS DRAINED FROM THE BOY
(UNTIL ONLY THE MAN REMAINS)

*

UNINVITED YOU LINGER AS BOUNDARY
(AND EYES)
SHE REPLIED TO THE BIRDS FROM HER DREAM
ARE YOU KIDDING?

*

INSTITUTIONAL SUFFIX
UPSIDE DOWN
I'M TAKING IT PERSONALLY
(ALTOGETHER PARALLEL)

*

MINDS ARE COLONIAL
YOU AND YOU AND YOU
ONE MAY DO WHATEVER ONE LIKES
I'M A PALINDROME

*

A LONGING FOR THE COMMON
YOU ARE MY EXAMPLE
I'M LOOKING AT THE MEADOW
THAT ONCE WAS HERE

*

THE FLAT SURFACE
THE WOUND'S ONLY RECOLLECTION
FLAT, ASEXUAL PARADOXES
WILL THERE EVER BE SILENCE?

*

THE PARTICULAR IN LANGUAGE
THERE'S NOTHING TO AGREE ON
I BARELY GRASP THE LEFTOVERS
OF THE POLITICS YOU CONSTRUCT

*

TRAFFIC OF CHARACTERISTICS
A SEVEN-YEAR CONTEXT GAP
HOPEFULLY HOPEFULLY
ALL IS WELL

*

TO LIVE YOUR LIFE IN FRONT OF THE SCREEN
A CREEK MEANDERING ACROSS THE PLAINS
RED DAWN WARFARE
HAVE WE HAD THIS CONVERSATION BEFORE?

*

SLEEP IS THE LANGUAGE OF OBLIVION
A SPACE OVERSHADOWING THE WILL
IT'S NOT A QUESTION OF JUSTICE
IT'S A QUESTION OF POWER!

*

INTEGRITY THAT TURNS INTO PARANOIA
AND THEN CEASES
THERE'S STILL PEOPLE
WHO BELIEVE IN EXCEPTIONS

*

EMERGENCY VEHICLE
CARBOHYDRATES, FAT, AND PROTEIN
HE SPEAKS AND SPEAKS UNTIL THEY STOP LISTENING
(AND ONLY HEAR HIS VOICE)

*

THE AGGREGATE OF TIME
FULL AND "EMPTY"
EVEN WHEN YOU HAVE NO WILL
YOU STILL HAVE RIGHTS

*

INFERNALLY THOROUGH
I AM REALISM
A CREDIBLE CENTER
SOON EVERYTHING WILL BE EXOTIC

*

STUPIDITY, KINDNESS
THE METAPHOR NULLIFIES THE BOUNDARY
(AND CLEARS THE GAME)
TO LOVE IS TO LOVE THEM ALL

*

EXTERNAL UNITS
GRADUALLY THE EMOTION WIDENS
SO THAT NOTHING MATTERS ANYMORE
NOT EVEN THE EMOTION

*

TO ALLOW ONESELF TO BE SEDUCED
TO BE COMPLETELY SATISFIED
I'M FULL
USA

*

THE CALLOSITY OF THE FRICTION AREA
MOST THINGS ARE THE SAME
I LIVE IN A WORLD THAT EXCEEDS
ALL SENSE AND IS WAY TO SIMPLE

*

TO BE STRONG AND HEARTY
THE LAST TRUE SPIRIT OF TIMES
DISTANT AND "COMPLETE"
WHAT IS IT YOU THINK YOU'LL UNDERSTAND?

*

I GREW UP IN A SORT OF PRISON
A DEVELOPMENTAL INSTITUTION
WITH DOUBLE LOYALTIES
OH YES, WELL NO

*

THE OPPOSITE OF MONUMENTS
ALL KNOWLEDGE EXISTS
YOU'RE VAGUE
COLD AND CARING

*

TO LOOK IN THE MIRROR
IS TO SEE ONE'S OWN BEGINNING
WE ARE REACHED BY A MESSAGE
WITHOUT A RINGTONE

*

FED IN ONE'S OWN RAREFICATION
YOU KNOW THE LIMITS
"SILENCE" EXCLUDES SILENCE
(AND SPEECH)

*

THE FRIGHT OF INTERRUPTION
THE ACTION TAKES PLACE OFFSTAGE
AT LAST
I FEEL SUPERVISED

*

US OR WE
HATRED FRATERNIZES
I ALMOST NEVER KNOW
TO WHOM I'M SPEAKING

¶

the sun being straight ahead   what
is no longer visible   complete
blackness   desolate gardens.
branches in bundles by walled
passages   it's the first science
low branches in amongst the
necklaces the belts   adjusting
to the climate   common formations
hide a peculiar nature   pure
fragments streaming to the scene
death in memoriam by the patterns
of the cell   spaces like paintings
a deathly pale day. a glimpse of
a dream   gradually roams about

thickets and shale the soil the hard
bronze   a silver powder thin enough
to be merged in the gold of outer
space. an opaque day where all is
emptied. a brain unveiled from its
conscience   a machine producing
themes. neither rope nor knife   just
not for you to possess or walk
around in or point at   we are all
here to die   the dusty steppe a joy
to behold   it moistens the eyes
a depthless volume passes by   we
greet one another as in a memory
the grey sun shines. heavy sky

lusterless air. a scenery of ice in
the distant   excessively rough
details. the musts of a material
way of life will find a natural
solution   one has to aim at the
heart   aim at these all the same
imprisoning walls   a streaming
ocean of patients hits the walls of
the institution   amongst them none
of the ill   only the living and the
dead. an extreme and rare sort of
regularity. the giver has conquered the
moment   sealed in rock. sentenced
to always see   all of you all the same

the camp all lit up   rapidly we eat
each one of us across from another
a general law called the principle of
cooperation   what is that blinking
light? a straight line   any action
filled with any kind of substance
being enacted during a single day
and striding pace by pace to come
to an end. outer space begins with
this blueprint   overturned it puts
everything in darkness. the leverage
divides into two sections. the
dynamics of the plot are revoked   the
conversation unfolds an item in the room

the vessels the bottles. a universe of
stereotypes where significance is
stored. the cliff uncovers a hall shrouded
in saffron   a palace of burning
copper. distant rays alongside limestone
and iron   for the first time we have
put the abstraction behind us. nothing
more regular than the synchronic order
the walls can't stop the sounds   they
enhance them. logic and psychology
plaited into a pattern   you learn to
fall asleep to all the outside noise. you
fall to your knees out of pain   the
production that won't be swapped

heaps to the roof. jewels diamonds
brilliants   the chilly hall that seals
the heart   it recalls of a dream the
prison had   tall columns and shadows
perishing into the wall   it's no use
looking for barbed wire   in the
barracks daylight filters through the
venetian blinds. crumbling units
sluggishly rampaging   a delightful
observation of the decay of the physical
figure. the curtain falls   page by page
plunging into a cloud of dust   lungs
breathe the stiff air. it isn't a voice of
its own   the stairs to the galley slaves

the sun can't break free yet   articulation
only of what can't be depicted by action
sheets with traces of bones loins
giddifying aluminium circles   a
partition of marbled glass   the
outskirts of cities reflected in thousands
of rainbows   a cascade erupts from
the eightieth floor   characters
praying crying   at the edge
surrounded by those who comfort. at
the foot of a quadrilateral tower. regular
wonders   the death of everyone
is a matter of course   saturable
colors of an impending horizon

those involved catch up with the
game without learning the rules   the
lavatory is a hole   a bedroom with
a pale textile carpet covering the
wooden floor   imprints sunken into
each brain   at the threshold the iron
of the lantern is on fire   the death
formidably mixed up in the circle of
everyday life   intervals of silence   a
generalization of the grammatical mood
in general. nothing to represent the
unbearable   the family tomb's location
i can't do anything for you. a room can
be empty and still drenched in light

TIME WHILED AWAY

curbed by school yard loudness   by
violence of passion   beauty countlessly
subjected to diverse economic systems
the days are flooded with endless shine
the monotony of doubled feelings
heavy froth of grapevines in the
moonlight pesticide   another night
falls over the world. the flare of clarity
burns the surface of the eye   the
hedge between the pages beams
beams   a linear story   its
description rests in the future. time
is a place of work   a dangerous
zone where powers are scrutinized

so you don't know why you are
here? one does know where one
is at. themes are converted into
unjustifications   indifference
dislike and finally repugnance
wrath   hate and fury
millstone vessels filling up with
sulfur. beyond the third dimension
intersected by a net of chains   a
mirror in a marble sink. a value
signalling the end   two beds   the
fugitive throws himself into the
crack. simultaneously morals and
linguistic habits are abandoned

¶

overabundance of materials
piled up until front doors can't be
opened   an opaque city shattered
by unprotective rituals   the elders
contemptuously frown on the
newly arrived   all slow hours
for whole days no one engages in
conversation. an absolutely wonderful
existence   it's a mania   boundaries
of the era   prison and refuge at the
same time   scattered notes on the
remnants of a system   units
mutually conditional on each other
it must be about five a.m.

a coup de théâtre on the stage of
things   to be able to see is a
circumstance   it's the scandal
of indifference   time is thirst
space is wrath   no forecasts
visionless hard staring eyes
not as a statement but a ban. on
April 16 finding oneself
released without explanations
unconditionally   in freedom   a
corridor   the tapestries shiver by the
main ropes   cell by cell   an archaic
architecture   hermetic actions   no
single act reveals what follows   next

every cliché as a silent understanding
every punctuation is meant to be where
it is. the prison of prisons   confined
without a core. why all this social
crystallization? seized with the
ecstasy of proper institutions   a
favorable position when it comes
to striking back at the assailants
the room is completed   thrown
into time   an organized descriptive
sequence intimately associated with
an instructive sequence   kicking
hitting with an iron pipe   burning
the neck with cigarettes

bodily prayer. fingers clasped   fists
clenched   alongside a tightly stretched
thread. façades of steel and extinct
hardwood   in the heart of the gap
the law secures a given order   the
world is public opinion   simultaneously
dread and alibi   in this respect all
freedom is an anomaly. civil servants
fixate their hands behind their backs and
carry through physical interrogations for
thirty six hours in a row   in a booth
predators pace to and fro   in the
mosaics hands of kings are sacrificed
the room being boiled through the image

you can't be let out since there is
no outside   hours separated by
meals and daily recess. an entirety
and a principle for classification
as if it were possible only to talk
about what is whole and functional
the hours of the day adds up to a
hole   black and white by turns
in the aperture   the taste of the
comprehensible is good   heaven's
peak   immense   the first room is far
elevated   over there   where you'll be
treated well. the forest embankment
is covered with a dazzling blanket

beaming generality. the cornered star
shines unaccompanied   it has
seized to live   the eyes are nature's
lamp   weary from prison   veiled
by tears. along the bars of apertures
the outside becomes a rhythmic field
a disturbed phenomenon of the
temporal   everything becomes
suspicious. the infinite is permanent
time isn't an agent for evolution
it is its golden frame   there is
infinity   that's all. the mass of
confinement which is viscous by
nature becomes a preservative factor

from the folds of the sheets a quiet
smile   in extinguished lament
between the outward time and the
inmate's time there's notification
time   and crime time   the
threshold of bars underneath an arch
of bones. birch beams facing oak pillars
by the vaguely shadowing backdrop
of sky   the absence of recognition
diminished in a second   lots of
mosquitoes   a corner for taking care
of one's needs   and a pitcher for
drinking and washing of hands   colossal
machines provide fluids for the gardens

the afternoon reclaims the world. at
the risk of suffocation confined within
oneself in the whole of nature   an
artificial structure   can it subsist?
exactly what occurs during these days?
the heat haze. still with the obligations
that come with the spoken word   the
prisoner revealed between letter and
object. a winter rain over a wall in
ruins   everything in its right place.
the synchronic order is general but
not imperative. common sense equals
the rhyme   to answer by shape
if one could only stay longer

Freke
Räihä

Gratinated pancake roulade with capers and champagne

Momentum—1.

It's impossible to make pancakes
without cracking a few eggs.

You crack a few eggs.

Try not to consider the amount:

Crowding, approved cannibalism
and fishmeal in the hen's fodder.

You wouldn't like to be pregnant
and all alone in the subway
eating staple commodities of similar standards.

Half a dozen is
the proper amount—Half of everything.

Momentum—2.

Cry over spilt milk.

You can comfort yourself with roses.

As much as;

You can reap these wounds:

Carbon dioxide permits,
depletion of farmland,
d i s p l a c e m e n t
of welfare means
Inevitably implied by this.

Weep a pair of buckets or so.

Momentum—3.

This will stir up all kinds of shit.
Stir.

Flour and salt.
Stir, Stir.

It's all about fractions of pints.
It's all about pinches of salt.

Stir, stir, roasting pan.

Momentum—4.

Oven.

the tool;

restrained power of 450 Farenheit.

You wait.

Put the ambience in position.
        The needle fits the engraved line.
            Surface noise, rhythms, recognition.

Momentum—5.

French style sour cream on;
—flower bud from the orchid of Salina

More salt/pepper.

Green-/Smoked-.

Now there's no way for you to skimp
you've come too far.

Roll it.

Momentum—6.

With cheese in oven:

It is grated, it blends in, over.

I'm repulsed by it
being stringy, beefy and extracted;
rewarding.

Production of malignant cells
may perfectly well occur in the defecation machinery;
laboratories and/or the man machine.

You're doing it behind closed door,
sometimes with the light turned off.

Momentum—7.

Champagne; from Champagne

Carbon dioxide is the faeces of microbes
they fatten themselves on the grape sugar
They form colonies

When the food is all gone
they can't migrate to other cells
such as humans/viruses.

They have no sufficient means of transportation.
They just die.

The dry juice
undergoes this process
on two occasions.

Filled with dualism;

We regard it as living matter
rather it is bottled ruins.

Gorgonzola pudding with port wine

Momentum—1.

The hen won't reestablish calcium
in as high a pace
as she is forced by us to make eggs.
It must be added.

A few of them with the balloon whisk.
Add only a handful of sugar.

Momentum—2.

This measurement of almonds in a mortar

Fill your hands
as you were to drink from a floating stream.

Which flows in a nice old movie.
Which flows past the hard-earned beach property.

Of which you can only dream
out of magazines.

You should dry your hands.

Momentum—3.

On top of that, a jug of cream.
40 %

Commodity food and
supply of A, D vitamins:
The sun only shines in summertime.

It's dark outside.
A darkness for some people
refracted only by ethyl alcohol.

Momentum—4.

A few table spoons of the wheat flour;
in with the balloon whisk again.

Be brutal;
perhaps with just as much
as can fit your hand.

Momentum—5.

The Gorgonzola weighs a pound.

Stir it into the liaison
You might first allow it to melt properly
As cheese should be served
tempered anyway.

The Gorgonzola being:
creamy green marble;

cow's milk with *Penicillium roqueforti*;
might cause symptoms such as nausea,
vomiting, diarrhea, and at its worst
attacks reminding of epileptic seizures.

In addition, molds shouldn't be accepted indoors.

Momentum—6.

It rests in the oven.
It rests for long in the oven.
It rests an eternal rest
   in pretty casserole
      perhaps lined with green flowers.

There's time for you to suggest a parlor game.

But you must lower the heat;
350 Fahrenheit.

That will do.

Momentum—7.

The wine is merely fermented a short minute.
Then becomes assassinated with grape spirit—
Hence living conditions are made impossible.

Preserving a sweetness
that contrasts with the salinity.

That's very efficient.

However, the publisher has discontinued its business.

1.
We don't accept unsolicited manuscripts.
We won't send any confirmation upon receiving a manuscript.
The Publisher can't be held accountable for any mishaps due to
the postal services.

We only accept manuscripts from poets who have read
a number of our published books
and who thereby consider themselves being either in sync with
our back list or unsurpassed by it.
And we'll get back to you as soon as possible.
At this moment we're not particularly interested in anything at all.

2.
We strive to give notice within three months
whether the book has been selected for publication or not,
but sometimes it might take longer.

We don't accept any floppy discs, or manuscripts by e-mail.
Unfortunately we can't accept manuscripts by e-mail
or on CD:s, but
we try to reply in writing
within three months.
(We won't open any files sent by e-mail.)

Don't forget your contact information
and kindly write a few lines about yourself.

3.
We only accept manuscripts in hard copy.
Currently, we don't publish any poetry.
However we gladly accept
comments, questions and good advice.

The publisher won't, for the time being, accept any
unsolicited manuscripts.
We accept manuscripts in printed format,
not by floppy disc, e-mail or fax.

We strive to give notice in 1-3 months,
whether the book has been selected for publication or not.

4.
We aim to give notice *after* two months or so

(during vacations the
turnaround time might be longer).

Have you written a novel or a collection of poetry?

Then you are welcome to send us your manuscript!

You're perfectly welcome to send your manuscript by e-mail but
we also accept manuscripts in hard copy.

However, no unsolicited manuscripts.

5.
Within two months we'll let you know our decision but
unfortunately we are unable to give any
elaborated comments
on rejected manuscripts.

Unfortunately we're not allowing for any manuscripts for the
time being.

Also bear in mind, we essentially won't publish any kind of poetry.

Finally we ask of you to be indulgent since it usually takes a few
months for us to give any decisive reply.

6.
We are currently suffering and are unfortunately
unable to take on any new writers.
Unsolicited material is sent at own risk.

It might take longer for us to reply.
For the time being we don't accept any manuscripts.

 This link is broken.

7.
We should in no way be held accountable for sent,
unsolicited manuscripts.

We publish our friends and perhaps
acquaintances to our friends.

All received manuscripts will end up unread in a
plastic bag
at the far end of a closet.

The manuscripts, concerning which we haven't agreed for you to send us, will immediately be burnt in the Publisher's oven without further notice.

We only accept manuscripts in paper format.

8.
We have a manuscript stop for the time being
since a whole lot of manuscripts have arrived in short time.

Thank you for all the exciting contributions!

Be careful enough to state your name and address.

We strive to reply in writing
after two months or so.

9.
Weekly we receive several manuscripts to take into consideration.
We receive a lot of contributions and are forced to screen firmly.

We receive a whole lot of manuscripts
and are unable to
give personal feedback on all of them.
We, this time, decline publication.

Conflict.

1.
We apologize for the delayed reply.
We have now read this [manuscript] but decided to decline
your kind offer of publication.
Unfortunately we have to turn down
the collaboration with you for publication.
We receive hundreds of contributions annually,
and are only able to go forward with a small fraction of those.

2.
Initially we would like to apologize for
not having replied earlier. Right now
we are only interested in publishing non-illustrated poetry col-
lections (in translation). In general we also scout for larger col-
lections, somewhere around at least 120+ pages for book pub-
lications. But you are welcome to resubmit at another time, in
order for us to give a second opinion.

I'm so sorry, I thought that I had already answered you.
                        [The manuscript] is a bit too "heavy" for us.

Thank you for your manuscript and please excuse our late reply,
we've had a stressful season.

3.
The particular, illustrative example:

We are so sorry to find out that you have submitted once already, and haven't got any reply, which we deeply regret. As you are certainly aware, the competition in the book market is tough, and for that reason we have to decline publication. Due to limited resources we are unfortunately unable to give any individual criticism.
(sic!)

12-22-2009 12:52 – 01-19-2011 12:49

4.
Unfortunately, this time we are unable to go forward with
your manuscript.
For the time being, there is no opportunity for us
to sign more writers this year.
We have already scheduled our
publications for a year ahead
and for the time being there is no economic leverage
to publish your manuscript. Moreover,
we will publish two poets
in the forthcoming year
and in order not to be a
too specialized publisher we unfortunately have to. (sic!)

5.
Submitted: (10/27/10):

It sounds exiting.
I'll get back to you with a detailed reply
next week.

Rejected: (3/31/11):

[We] have read your manuscript and found it to be pretty good, but, unfortunately.

6.
Right now we can't see any possibility to publish
your poems.
We have received a few turns of texts from you and
we have had a look at all of them and
we decline publication,
we simply couldn't take a liking to the texts.

7.
We appreciate your continued support and your purchase
of our books.
Unfortunately we couldn't find any room for your work
in this issue.
Sometimes this happens. Feel no despondency.
Comfort yourself with nostalgia,
fondly recall the innocent, previously perverted acts
in the pasture.
We do.
But honestly I don't think there is
very much for him[1]
to say about this in the annotations.
Good luck with the publication!

---

[1] The world's leading biographer on the subject is
declared incompetent by [A literary agency].

8.
Unfortunately we don't have any possibility to publish them.
Unfortunately we have decided not to publish them.

Unfortunately we need to decline publication.
Unfortunately we need to decline publication.
Unfortunately we need to decline publication.
Unfortunately we need to decline publication.

Unfortunately we have now reached the decision to
decline publication.
Unfortunately there is no possibility to have it published
in our publishing house.

9.
Thank you for your request and
we wish you all luck
in finding an alternate home for this work.

Thank you for the submitted texts
and your interest in the magazine.

Unfortunately we have decided not to print your contribution.
Unfortunately we can't go forward with it this time.

The space for poetry has shrunken somewhat.

1.
Confidentiality clause;

The information contained in this message is for the intended recipient(s) only. All illegitimate use of this e-mail message by storage on any unit with the purpose of copying or spreading it, without a preceding permission from the copyright owner, is strictly forbidden:

We wish you good luck in finding an alternate home for this work.

2.
Hence it is not on behalf of quality that I after all
—at long last—now decline the publication.

Moreover it's actually
a very interesting manuscript you have presented to us,
existential, literary, poetologic,
conceptual, social. The touch of pataphysics
relieves
[...]
the rather heavy themes. Both
[its] hysterical exhilaration and
profound despair appear to be genuine.

Or;

1.

This letter won't reach you. Unfortunately we haven't read your manuscript and probably won't do so either. And the way things stand it's not likely that we would answer your letter, your phone calls, your emails. Basically we have no resources for that, you see: there is something gruesomely true about the mechanism that controls us. We are not here, we are on vacation, we need a wages agreement, we are on strike. There's no need for you to be upset, we no longer read any manuscripts, we can't read, we prefer to do poor translations and ignore postage rates. We'll make a cut-up of his latest book/her latest images and reel it off as if it was methadonical psychomorphs.

2.

Nor is it important from where we actually get it, you won't get to know it. You'll have to wait. You won't get to know it if you'll get to know it. We are controlled by the truth; resources, ideals, those one finds coarse or the love of books. This letter won't reach you. Sure, you might say that no one can fuck a book, and thereby it neither can be loved. I agree, but not my wife, who doesn't own a single copy of you or your love. We have changed our phone number, address, surname, ISBN and place of publication. You can reach me at the printing house. We have changed printing house. We are on vacation, we have altered our vacations, we have replaced vacations with industry. We have changed owners, language, currency and/or government—which regulates the bits, the bytes and the hexagonal source code of the domain. We have no contracts, no responsibility. We only have the dwelling coffee grounds in the refreshment room. Unfortunately we are not able to, you are one out of many. This letter won't reach you.

Matilda Södergran

¶

A burgundy tranquility shuts the eye.

I'm bleeding sheets and delis.
Leaving streamingly leaving the body leaving

the membrane, falsely gold impressed.

Sweeping the floor with india ink.

Pitfalls.

¶

Tears hanging as ragged dough
from the domes

you may shed the relief
too heavy to bear.

You see it, death throes are far below,
one more last time.

How you always know that you've already seen it
and that you'll see it again.

You'll see it again.

¶

Sifting
confectioners' sugar
through
the scalp.

One
inch
and
I
still
don't
know
how
it
feels
to
hit
the sky.

¶

Defend myself against your air raids.

My legs cramp in your intoxicated throat, no, not exactly as were before,
more as is now, when underfed neighborhoods of concrete spread the
salinity,
the revolution

and I tear all your loose ends, draping my pearl covered torso,
injecting the incomprehensible into hip bones, ribs,

empty bowls.

Gagged I choke, standing still.
Pulling myself across tree trunks, bark under my skin.

Turn me face down and look into my split open Cyclopes' eye,
pull the night sky off of me, peel off the powerlessness.

Surgeries. All went black.

¶

She is dispersed in the ant-heap,
allowing the six-footed ones to crawl into her.

A stench of piss and ant breath.

She is carefully dressed
to make pretence of a freshness, softness,

and there is something clinical and bitter
about the wrinkles in her lips.

Yesterday he kissed her.
Aimed.

¶

Embalmed, I wait in the trees,
juicy fruits, the blushing positioned inside of me.

You think you know exactly where you have me,
a body dispersed in the areolae.

If I get wet from the amniotic fluid of the sky

as if someone up there spreads her legs
as if someone wants to give birth to somebody else on top of me,

then I put an unrestrained smile on, knowing that
these wringing motions won't be covered.

¶

1. Your mouth is very open.

I burst in with the entire length of my body.
See the spider eggs in your throat, how the web finds its way

further down.

2. I wear a tight necklace of high pulse.

Soon   I'll   be   tightened   further.

¶

The catheter inserted to the brain. In certain spots it
releases fluids that have flooded the space for thoughts.

A yellow mood

ties me to the flow.
I'm a spectator in these crude games.

There are things that always streams.
There are catheters inserted in urethras,
meninx, and lips.

Fluids necessary to be extracted.

¶

Each night the shady teats in your face are being milked.
No one would attempt to drink

the whites.

I think I never noticed when what is separating us was
breeded in your man-womb. How afterwards you bled.

How aware we actually were in the lamplight.

There are units of measurement drawn on your abdomen
and each night I smear ointment on them when you are asleep

wishing for them to go away.

¶

It
was
a
bird
who
grew
tired
and
accidentally
you
just
stood
there
with
a
knife

and a bag empty of wings.

¶

The braille on my mons veneris is illegible.
Impossible to decipher.

You shall not name me. You shall not swell.

Birds are crawling in the sediments.
The bottle of solvent. Colors shed.

Your hands are milking me.
The birds' beak encloses my nipples.

You shall not worship, your life is lost in me.

There's an animal-headed cold child
being silenced tonight.

¶

My love
is an undernourished liver between my legs.

Adapts a decreasing oblivion.

Ten days of stuffed soil in my cavities.
Ten days of the sea clay on my floor.

I forget, easily I forget.

¶

You tried to speak through the gag.

You interfered.

You don't know what's the matter with you.

Then you dream. The thin stockings always break.

The ladders tear long lines.

You forget to undress. You forget to sleep.

Each fabric itch like skin.

¶

You are evident to his gaze, his composure.

Your whole body is stripped of hair.

Strand by strand. All hair is removed.

Is it relevant for you to ask questions.

¶

Fresh air. A breeze. From you not a sound.

You think of beetles.

The shell on their backs.

¶

You climb in birds. Their abdomens are absinthe.

Your mouth is full. Hayey.

You graze. You are not the only one to unlikely be here.

Behaving like cattle and hardly bird-like.

Am I right to give this description?

¶

Your nipples move across the body.

You never find them when the child is hungry.

When starving.

¶

All your hands are whores.

All your solid grounds are soulless.

The tongue races through tangled hair.

Are your kisses supposed to symbolize some kind of dignity afterwards?

Justify your behavior if you can.

¶

The candles are burnt out in the chandelier hanging from your anus.

You don't belong here. You can't hear the prisms shatter.

¶

They all want to beautify you.

You're not ready.

¶

The brain is pulled out to be thoroughly examined.

You lack references on how to behave:

> You wear your face over your crotch.

> Cross the field diagonally.

> Fall into the dry wheat.

> You chose a path normally you wouldn't have.

> Everything is yellow. You chew the air like froth.

> It is sometimes hard to think about the laughter of a next-of-kin.

¶

Lame. Desireless. You thought you needed a face.

Your hair turns black. Your body turns dark.

A commencing decay.

A whore has thrown open the gates in you.

Scratch here. Scratch there. Scratch yourself open.

You wear your crotch over your face. (or the other way around)

⁋

To introduce another person to your longing.

A smell of salt comes through the open window.

You eat old fruit. Paint your lips.

Observe the way he leaves the apartment.

¶

You grab the tongue with both hands pulling like crazy

(clearly you know it isn't yours).

www.ingramcontent.com/pod-product-compliance
Lightning Source LLC
Chambersburg PA
CBHW020404130626
46549CB00006B/2431